YOU
NEED
TO
SUCCEED

By Glenda Feilen

Ten Habits
YOU NEED
TO SUCCEED

Starquest Inc.

Successful People
Do the Same
Things
No Matter What
Business
They Are In!

ISBN: 0-9755674-4-6

First Edition published 2004

Printed in the United States of America

http://www.areallyourpiecesinplace.com

Address for information:
Starquest Inc.
P.O. Box 2218
El Cajon, CA 92021

ABOUT THE AUTHOR

Glenda Feilen graduated from college with a BA degree in Russian. After teaching high school Russian and English in Salt Lake City, she spent several years as a buyer for the largest chain store in Las Vegas, Nevada. Because of a life-threatening illness, Glenda began her studies in the holistic health field, which enabled her to return to excellent health. After earning several holistic degrees, she opened an office in San Diego and maintained that practice for 13 years, with a three-to six-month waiting list for a consultation. For twenty-one years she has been an international marketing director for a health-focused corporation, lecturing all over the world on nutrition and personal development. She earned a law degree and enjoys studying law as a hobby. Glenda's daughters are her pride and joy - all five graduated from college and are successful in their own lives.

TABLE of CONTENTS

Chapter 1

THERE IS A PATTERN
TO SUCCESS

Success does not just happen. It is the result of *specific success principles and skills* applied to a given situation. These principles may be applied consciously or unconsciously; either way, when you follow the pattern for success you receive a certain result, whether or not you're aware of the pattern. If you want success, find successful people, see what they do, and COPY THEIR ACTIONS. You'll find that successful people do exactly the same things and have specific characteristics in common. This is no accident. Certain qualities and characteristics are required for success. There is no negotiating, because the universe sets the requirements and they aren't multiple choice. They must *all* be met.

Success is as simple as following

1

these universal rules, just as nature does. When you plant wheat, you reap wheat. If you plant corn but wish for wheat, you still reap corn. You can wish for wheat, hope for wheat, talk to your corn seeds at midnight, hire an expert horticulturist at great expense, but all that extra effort is a waste of time. Growing wheat requires planting wheat, then following through on important tasks such as watering, weeding, and harvesting your crop.

If you want to visit a town on the east side of an island, you must take the road going east. If you take the road going west you won't reach the desired town. You'll either have to settle for something you don't want *or* change your direction. So it is with success—follow the rules, take the right road, and you'll get there!

Chapter 2

ACTION IS A VERB

The greatest mistake a man can make is doing nothing.   *John Maxwell*

You've probably heard the saying, "attitude is everything." That is absolutely not true. Another "A" word is necessary for success: ACTION. You can sit in your chair on the beach day after day with a wonderful attitude, but if you don't take specific actions to accomplish your goal, you will *not* achieve it.

Action is a vital key to success. Your success in life is directly related to how much action you take. Some people take *no action;* they just talk about doing things. Others take *a little action* until they accomplish some degree of success (even though they haven't reached their desired goal).

 The most successful people enjoy the challenge of taking *as much action as possible* and never stop, because they actually enjoy the action. Which are you?

3

Unsuccessful *no-action* people procrastinate. They use the word *try*. Now that's a joke! How can someone TRY? It's impossible to try. What exactly does TRY mean? Does it mean you aren't going to do something, but you don't want to admit it? Yes, that's it!

Really now, try to pick up a glass of water. You either decide to pick it up and DO it, or you decide not to, and DON'T. So, what is try? It's stupidity. No sane person would say the word and mean it, because it's meaningless. It's absurd! If someone tells you he or she will *try,* you know that's just an excuse and he has no intention of taking action. Try is a word people hide behind. Next time you catch yourself saying the word *try,* get real and commit one way or the other to either take action or not to take action.

Those who take *a little action,* do as much as they feel is necessary to rationalize their future inaction. They're either unmotivated because they don't believe in the desired goal, or they have no compelling reason to accomplish the tasks. Usually when individuals take only a little action and then stop, it's because they do just enough toward their desired goal to stay within their comfort zone. When they reach a point that puts them in stress, they stop moving forward. Continued success requires that you LIVE OUTSIDE YOUR COMFORT ZONE. Only when you challenge yourself by doing things that make you uncomfortable are you growing. You can only expand your possibilities when you expand your comfort circle. Only by doing and feeling things you've never experienced before, can you make it possible to do more than you've ever done before. Look around you and think of at least two people who've stayed in the same life situation for years. Can you imagine those people stepping out and doing something new and different? Of course not. If they could, they would have changed their circumstances. Each time you do something outside your comfort level you expand your circle of comfort. If you continue taking such actions, you become limitless. Fear is the only thing that will stop you from moving out of that imaginary cage you've put yourself in.

Many unsuccessful people think successful people don't have the fear that stops them in their tracks. Wrong! People who

5

take all the action required still have the fear, but they take action anyway. By taking action, they come to realize the fear was unwarranted, or at least exaggerated. By taking action they expand their comfort zone. They feel the gratification of forward movement. Continued expansion of their comfort zone creates momentum, and each new action they take comes from a new expanded place. Soon, the actions become a challenge; they're enjoyable and stimulating. Successful people play a game with themselves. They put themselves in challenging situations and learn to enjoy resolving the challenge. Successful people know that if you want something you've never had, you have to do something you've never done. Because risk equals rewards and moving out of your comfort zone is always a risk, these people frequently receive the rewards of success. The bigger the risk— the greater the reward!

EVEN IF YOU'RE ON THE RIGHT ROAD, IF YOU'RE NOT MOVING— YOUR'E GOING NOWHERE!

Will Rogers

Life is a DO it yourself program. DO is an action word. It indicates movement. Without action, don't expect success. What's the difference between successful people and unsuccessful people? Successful people DO what unsuccessful people won't do.

There was a time when I found salesmen in my territory weren't producing because they weren't making the necessary contacts. During one of our sales meetings I had a basketball hoop set up and each salesperson received a basketball when they arrived. A few people took a shot and put the ball down. Some gave the ball back and said it wasn't their thing; they didn't even try—indicating it was too hard for them or they weren't in the mood. Some people shot until they made a basket. A few of them even wanted to try again and again to see how many times they could be successful. So it is in life.

Wayne Gretsky said: "100% of the shots you don't take, don't go in." Some people won't even make the effort to score in life. Others will give it a try but soon quit. Some people find the mere *effort* exhilarating and enjoy the journey as much as they enjoy reaching the goal. The fact remains, if you don't shoot, you won't score. If you don't make the effort, you won't reap the rewards!

If you don't feel like it, DO IT ANYWAY! That's a secret successful people know, and unsuccessful people don't want to know.

Chapter 3

INTENTIONS DON'T COUNT

Intentions don't count! Intentions are ideas without action, but they are not substitutes for action. They're just the *starting point* for every good thing. Some people excuse themselves from success because they had good intentions. "Oh well, I had good intentions." Ever heard that one? Everyone has intentions. Life is made up of them, some good, some bad, but the actions we take is what creates success in life—or not! You must learn to measure life by results, not by intentions. Good intentions without taking the correct action will lead you nowhere.

People don't care about your intentions. They care about what you do. Your boss doesn't care if you *meant* to contact your sales leads. Your professor doesn't care if you *meant* to do your homework. The IRS doesn't care if you *meant* to pay your taxes. Actions make the difference! Actions create success.

Everyone has ideas. They're a dime a

dozen and they pop into our heads when we least expect them. The problem is, few people bother taking *action* on their ideas in order to accomplish success. Most people don't even pick up a pencil and paper and write down those incredible ideas that pop into their heads. And unfortunately, they're rarely given to us more than once!

One of the greatest mistakes about being successful is the idea that you should feel good or feel motivated before *you act*. Never wait to feel motivated! Motivation almost always follows action, but seldom precedes it. Emerson said, "Do the thing and you shall have the power." Champions commit to disciplined actions and pay little attention to how they feel. George Zalucki in *Profile of a Champion* tells us that mastery comes through tedious repetition of the principles and rules of the game you're playing. The game you're playing is LIFE and every day is Super Bowl Sunday!

If you don't feel like doing something, DO IT ANYWAY! The secret successful people know is that you can't wait for the feeling that creates the desire for you to take action; you take the action *even though you don't feel like it—and miracu-*

lously the feeling will follow!

ACTION PRECEDES MOTIVATION!

It's not what you do that matters, it's what you get done!

You don't have to be
good to start,
but you do have to
start to be good.

**The best way to get
things done
is to begin.**
Horace Greeley

Do the thing and you
shall have the power;
but they who do not the
thing have not the power.

Chapter 4

HOW DO YOU
MEASURE SUCCESS?

There's ONLY ONE WAY to measure success—results! The *only* way to measure success is based on bottom line results. It doesn't matter whether you're selling nails, playing football, or taking a college class; whatever you produce is the bottom line. There's only one pathway to achieving results for any given task:

- Decide specifically on the result you want: **YOUR GOAL.**
- Decide specifically on what you need to do to get that result: **YOUR ACTION PLAN.**
- Decide to **DO IT.** You're never going to create momentum without action.
- **EVALUATE** your progress.

As you take action, if you find it actually takes more than you thought to get the desired result, decide in advance to do *whatever* it *takes*. *That's* how you get the result you want. If you don't have an action plan, you're not going anywhere. If you don't have a goal, you'll go through life living other people's goals.

Most people don't get what they want in life because they don't *know* what they want in life. They haven't taken the time to actually write it down. So it is with any goal you desire. When you embark on a plane trip, you need a flight plan if you're going to arrive at the desired destination. First, you must decide on a destination and when you plan to arrive. That's your GOAL. Secondly, you determine a plan based on experts who've successfully flown to that destination. Smart people find others who've succeeded at the *exact task* and *do exactly the same.* They've paved the path for you. They've already done the hard work. There's nothing brilliant about discovering this information all over again. The brilliance is in using the information and applying it to your *specific set of circumstances* as your ACTION PLAN.

As you fly, winds and turbulence can knock you off course and you make adjustments to stay within the flight plan. Flexibility is a must, so don't be afraid to make slight changes to your action plan in order to accomplish your goals. Every pilot knows that variables occur. If the pilot didn't continuously evaluate his position, he wouldn't know adjustments need to be made, and so it is with you. Take time to *evaluate* your actions and see if you're still on track or if adjustments need to be made in your action plan. Turbulence happens—so do this frequently!

THE MOST VALUABLE HABIT

Once your goal is crystal clear and you have an action plan, all that's left is to *do it*. A wise man who is the leader of millions said, "Do it! Do it right! Do it right now!" The only big question left to discuss is *what* to do. Many people fill their hours with actions that don't take them towards their goals. There's a simple remedy for this problem.

A famous man offered to improve the profits of a company, and he stipulated they wouldn't need to pay him a salary or fee for his services up front.

The company would pay him according to how much they felt he'd benefited them. By using the simple technique, which he taught, the company's profits soared and the employees saw benefits not only at work, but in their personal lives. This technique will do the same for you. Needless to say, the man received an amount that far exceeded even his expectations.

Here's the technique:

- Every night before you go to bed make a numbered list *by priority (the most important things first)* of the six to eight things you must do the next day which directly move you forward to your goal.
- The next day begin at the TOP of the list and accomplish the tasks one by one.
- Do not skip to the next number until the previous task been completely accomplished.

Here's an example:

---

1. **Exercise**

2. **Take kids to school**

3. **Check messages and respond**

4. **Make calls to set up appointments**
   a) Mary C.   b) Tyler J.   c) Chris W.
   d) Mark P.   e) Debbie S.

5. **Read new update from company**

6. **Write and e-mail newsletter to directors**

7. **Make sales calls:**
   a) 12:00: PM Tom—lunch
   b) 3:00 Clark H.
   c) 5:00 Larry V.

**IF YOU DON'T DO IT—
YOU WON'T DO IT**

You can take workshops and training seminars, read books, and gorge yourself with knowledge from every source. But if you don't put that knowledge into action, YOU HAVE NO POWER. To have it and not use it makes you no better off than the ignorant person who doesn't know better. This is frequently the difference between success and failure. Many people *know* what to do, but they DON'T DO IT. They choose to fail.

KNOWLEDGE is POWER!
Wrong!

IMPLEMENTATION of KNOWLEDGE is POWER!

Chapter 5

BE PERSISTENT!

The race is not always won by the fastest, most skilled, or most qualified. Sometimes the race is won by those who keep on running.

Who doesn't know about the race between the tortoise and the hare? Anyone putting money on who would win would be crazy to bet on the slow but persistent tortoise. We all know the hare has the ability to quickly arrive at the goal line and leave the tortoise in the dust. But having the ability doesn't always mean you'll get the prize. Often, those who 'have the ability' aren't focused on the goal line and get side tracked. The slow but persistent arrive to collect their success because they knew where they were going and *didn't lose focus.* Slowly, but **surely**, is often the way to success, although there's nothing wrong with being fast *and* focused if you want to get there first!

Be persistent. Show up. Do the thing that needs to be done and keep on doing it! You will be rewarded. The universe knows what it takes. Keep doing what needs to be done until you get there! *You* don't decide when that is. The universe does. The universe will test you and when it figures out you are WILLING to do whatever it takes, it suddenly doesn't require it of you. But, you can't fool the universe. You really must be WILLING to do whatever it takes.

Mickey Mantle said, "During the eighteen years I came to bat almost 109,000 times. I struck out about 1,700 times and walked maybe 1,800 times. You figure a ball player will average about 500 at-bats a season. That means I played seven years in the major leagues without even hitting the ball."

Babe Ruth who is known as the greatest home-run hitter, also holds the greatest strike-out record.

Henry Ford went broke five times before he succeeded.

Be persistent!

THERE IS A DIFFERENCE BETWEEN BEING PERSISTENT AND BEING CONSISTENT

You've probably been told that being consistent is important to success. What if you have a strategy that isn't working? Are you going to keep doing it over and over again, hoping next time will be different? Many people don't realize that if what they're doing doesn't work, they need to find what *does* work and *then* be consistent.

There's a big difference between rats and humans. In a maze, rats will quickly learn which way does *not* get them to their destination and never go that way again. Humans just keep going down the same path over and over again, even if it isn't productive. If something doesn't work, approach it differently. Don't think you've failed. Failure is nothing more than finding one more way something doesn't work and getting closer to what does work. Just try something different.

Once you find out what works, being consistent is vital. Look at McDonalds. Whether it's Hong Kong, Russia, Costa Rica or San Diego, you know what to expect and people go there because of it. The fast-food chain found out what worked and are consistent!

**THE GREATEST THING
IN THIS WORLD
IS NOT SO MUCH
WHERE WE ARE
BUT IN WHAT
DIRECTION WE ARE MOVING**

Oliver Wendell Holmes

Chapter 6

STRIVE FOR EXCELLENCE

"The quality of a person's life is in direct proportion to their commitment to excellence, regardless of their field of endeavor."
Oliver Wendell Holmes

Excellence can be attained by consistently striving for perfection. You may have heard that "practice makes perfect." Not so! *Perfect* practice makes perfect! Strive for perfection from the beginning, whatever your field of endeavor. Practice without improvement is meaningless. A Pop Warner coach was right when he said, "You play the way you practice." As you make mistakes, recognize them and continually improve until you've achieved excellence. Mediocrity is acceptable to the world. Don't allow it be acceptable to you. If you care enough to invest a valuable moment of your life to do something, then you should care enough to make that moment count and do your very best. It won't always be perfect, of course, but keep STRIVING. When you strive for excellence, you gradually become better and better. The best may be only a miniscule better than everyone else. A racehorse who wins the pot isn't hundreds of times faster than the rest of the pack. He's often just a nose better. The horse wouldn't have won if someone hadn't been striving for excellence.

Your only limitations are those set up in your own mind.

**Every job
is a
self
portrait
of the
person
who did it.**

There is no use
in walking five miles
to fish
when you can depend
on being as successful
near home.

Mark Twain

Chapter 7

KNOW THE DIFFERENCE BETWEEN DREAMS and GOALS

Unlock your success by knowing the difference between dreams and goals. DREAMS are pie in the sky. They're balloons that float in and out of your mind. They are as wispy and intangible as clouds. Yet dreams are wonderful. A successful man once told me that the problem with people is they don't dream big enough.

However, true success only *begins* with dreams! So how *do* dreams relate to success? If you want to be successful, you must take those dreams and turn them into goals. You must take those pie in the sky dreams and bring them down to earth. GOALS are dreams with a deadline and an action plan (with specific dates, specific dollar amounts, and

27

specific actions with specific people). Your ACTION PLAN is your map. It tells you where you're going and when you will get there. Sure, you may need to make changes in that action plan, but if you don't *have* a plan, you aren't going anywhere. If *you* don't *have* a goal, you'll go through life living other people's goals.

Many people think they can just dream about what they want and someday, through some stroke of luck, or even their own hard work, those dreams will manifest in their lives. I say to them, "Dream on!" But remember, those dreams must become concrete. They must be written down with a specific plan. Once you realize your dreams can be accomplished by turning them into goals with set timelines, write a specific *long term goal* and an *immediate short term goal* that you can monitor daily or weekly. Then, based on the dead lines you've chosen, plan exactly where you have to be when you're one quarter, one half, and three quarters of the way to your final deadline on both the long and short term goal. Along with that information, make a detailed action plan to implement your goals.

Dreams can come true if you know what to do with them! Get your dreams out of your head and on paper so they seem more real to you. Define them with specifics, such as: when, where, how much, and with whom they'll be accomplished. Then, on the back of your goal paper, write the most important information of all—the reason WHY you're attaining the goal. What will you have that you don't have now? How will you feel differently than you feel now? How will achieving this goal benefit you? Is it worth it? If not, come up with a more compelling reason. If you don't have a good reason, you won't bother to do what it takes to reach the goal.

A man dreamed every day (as he drove to work, at work, and frequently in his spare time) of starting his own company. He was amazed at how quickly this long-term dream came true when he actually wrote down how different his life would be if the dream became a reality. The writing down process actually spurred an emotion in him that simply dreaming had never given him. He was so inspired that he put himself on a strict timeline, faithfully kept to his plan, and today is a successful man with a profitable business. Best of all—he has the lifestyle he'd always dreamed of.

Never In history
when you've missed the
target
has it been
the target's fault.

**AIM AT NOTHING
AND YOU'LL
PROBABLY HIT IT.**

Chapter 8

GAIN RAPPORT WITH ANYONE

When I think about gaining rapport, I automatically think of martial arts. Picture two martial artists posed against one another. When they both charge, they can go on and on without either one making progress. However, an incredible move can create an instant winner. When one of them moves toward the other and aligns with them, he easily redirects the energy to move both of them in his direction, scoring a win. When you align yourself with the other person's position, that person automatically follows you back to yours.

There are three easy steps to gain rapport with anyone. There are three forms of communication:
    1) words
    2) how you use your voice
    3) the way you use your body.

When you're communicating with someone, copy them by using similar words, voice tones, and physiology. This aligns you with them. Once they know you understand them, they're willing to look at your point of view.

When you feel yourself preparing to lock horns with someone, remember it is more profitable if you lock hands instead.

-Napoleon Hill

PEOPLE LIKE PEOPLE WHO ARE LIKE THEM— SO BE LIKE THEM!

1) WORDS

To gain rapport with another person, listen for *special key words* he uses to illustrate his point of view. Use *his key words* when discussing the situation with him. Use similar *content* when going over facts. Use *common experiences* to illustrate that you understand where the other person is coming from.

Sales people have known this for years. A real estate person who's heard the buyer say that he'd just like to "chill out" when he comes home from work, will tell the buyer the sitting room is a "perfect place to chill out after work". The buyer will then think, "Wow, this person gets me! He must be just like me!" and therefore be open to buying the house, since it's such a great place to chill out. Successful sales people know that a few of those personally meaningful words connected to their products will bring buyers closer to being their friend and buying from them.

2) HOW YOU USE YOUR VOICE

Match your voice to the other person's

* volume
* speed

If they speak slowly, match their speed, even if it isn't normal for you. If you whiz through the conversation at the speed of light, there will be no rapport—only irritation. If they speak loudly, you should do the same. Will they notice? Will they know you're doing this? NO—because you're matching them, not mimicking them. The only thing they'll notice is that you're like them.

A friend told me she couldn't relax around a common acquaintance. I was surprised to hear this and asked what she felt the problem was. She quickly answered, "She talks so fast and loud that I always have to be thinking or concentrating when I'm around her. Sometimes, I'd just like to have a pleasant conversation with her." The lady who had felt pressured by the fast speaking friend was a slow paced, intelligent, but conscientious woman who felt obligated to keep up with her friend's conversations. To do so was taxing to her, even to the point of not associating with the lady. The fast-speaking acquaintance probably wonders why her friend is avoiding her and would gladly slow her words and quiet her voice if she only understood the problem.

3) THE WAY YOU USE YOUR BODY

The way you use your body represents over 50% of what actually influences people when you communicate. That's right—actions mean more than words! Therefore, when you communicate with someone it's important to mirror his body language. Are his arms crossed? Is he holding a pen? If so, inconspicuously move toward matching his gestures: cross your arms or pick up a pen and hold it like the other person. Does the other person use a certain *gesture* as he speaks? So—go for it. How does he *stand?* What is his facial *ex-pression?* Does he appear *relaxed or tense?* Do what he does. He won't realize you're mirroring his gestures—he'll just know he feels great rapport with you.

Once you gain the other person's confidence, you may bring him toward your side or point of view. Practice this; become an expert, and watch your life change. The world is filled with people. All the money you're ever going to have is in their pockets and you won't get it until you gain rapport with them.

Gaining rapport with these three techniques is not only effective, it's fun to see how quickly it works.

PEOPLE LIKE PEOPLE WHO LIKE THEM— SO SHOW THEM YOU LIKE THEM!

How do people know you like them?
- You *compliment them*; you catch them doing something right.
- If you like them, you *listen to them* without interrupting.
- You show sincere *interest* in them.

S M I L E S
are reciprocal.
If you want one, give one away!

There is only one rule
for learning to be a
good talker,
Learn how to listen.

-Christopher Morley

You can make more friends
in two months
by becoming interested
in other people
than you can
in two years
by trying to get other people
interested in you.

-Dale Carnegie

**Success is 99%
luck.
Ask any failure.**

Chapter 9

HOW CAN I GET "LUCKY"?

You can wake up lucky every day. Luck happens when opportunity meets preparation! People make their own luck by taking advantage of every opportunity that presents itself to them. One person can see a glass half full and another sees it half-empty. Likewise, one person can see an opportunity and recognize it as just that, while another views the same opportunity as a problem. A 1996 high school graduate in California stated it this way:

Some people throw stones;
Some people stumble over them;
Some people climb over them;
Some people build with them.

SUCCESSFUL PEOPLE DO WHAT UNSUCCESSFUL PEOPLE CHOOSE NOT TO DO!

Unsuccessful people choose to fail.

Chapter 10

CHANGE IS A CONSTANT

Nothing is permanent
except change.

There's an old saying, "The only thing that's constant in life is change." Because this is true, it's easy to be distracted by our constantly changing world and take our eyes off our goals. Frequently we not only resist change; we fear it.

We should welcome change. A motivational poster pictured a long road on one side of mountain with a large turn and a long road on the other side of the mountain. It was entitled: CHANGE—A bend in the road isn't the end of the road....UNLESS you fail to make the turn. We mustn't resist the twists and turns that present themselves as we travel our daily roads to success.

There is a small gold sign on my desk that says:
OUR POLICY, RIGID FLEXIBILITY

Napoleon Hill states in *LAW OF SUCCESS* that life resembles a great kaleidoscope. It's ever changing but continually beautiful.

There is a secret little word that keeps me  sane, nice, and successful. This key unlocks the door that stops success in its tracks. It's so important because I must do it thousands of times a day. Ready? AD-JUST!

We have literally hundreds of chances to adjust every day. For example, when your alarm clock doesn't go off, your appointment cancels as you're walking out the door, or someone cuts you off while driving. You simply adjust or *you* will be the loser.

All of us are constantly adjusting; if not, we have a difficult time in life. The ability to flow with life, with relationships, and with the changing business world helps make us successful. People who are not flexible consider themselves to be victims of change. You choose to be a victim when you don't adjust. *It's not what happens in* *life (or business); **it's how you take it!***

    Younger people seem to adjust more easily to changes. A saying that used to be popular with teenagers when a person was rambling about something that happened was, "Get over it!" What good advice! Why make a mountain out of a molehill? Why turn your dollars into pennies? Why destroy a relationship? Why stop your success, when you can simply ADJUST?

HE

Who laughs...

LASTS

Tim Hansel

Chapter 11

GIVE YOURSELF A CHEER!

If you don't celebrate your successes, are they really successes?

You should always give yourself a cheer when you reach a milestone on the road to your goal. Why? Because it helps you realize how much you've progressed. Secondly, you'll want to have more success so you can continue celebrating. All work and no play really does make life a bore. Everyone deserves some play and if you don't take advantage of small successes, you lose the joy of success. Third, you will work harder and more effectively toward your goal after you've nurtured and appreciated yourself and your accomplishments.

Give yourself a hug! Say nice things to yourself! Have a special night out on you! You deserve it.

It takes just as much
time and energy
to wish
as it does to plan.

Chapter 12

THE UNIVERSAL GOLDEN RULE

The golden rule of the universe is one that no one can circumvent. What happens in any person's life is exactly what he has puts out to the universe. You are a broadcasting and receiving station. What you broadcast outward in thoughts, feelings, words, and actions, you receive back in kind. Every thought you think, every emotion you feel, every word you say, and every action you take has its counterpart in some circumstance you will eventually encounter.

You cannot act a certain way toward another person without first thinking a thought. That thought has become part of your *own* subconscious (creative) mind and has an effect on the person you become. Therefore, you can't afford to hate another person, because that very emotion you sent out will return to you. On the other hand, what a great advantage it is when you send messages of support, cooperation, acceptance, generosity, and love to others. You are ordering these things back into your life. When you understand this universal law, you understand that it's you who induces others to act toward you the way you want them to act—by adjusting *your* attitude toward them.

To understand this rule is to know that every sales person will only be successful when he or she truly believes in the benefits of his product or service. Every teacher can only persuade others if he or she is convinced of the philosophy they're putting forth. Every person in a relationship can only receive the response he or she wants from the other person when it's unconditionally given first.

You are the "master of your fate" and the "captain of your soul" because you have the power to control your own thoughts, feelings, words, and actions, and create whatever circumstances you want in your life.

WHAT YOU GET IS WHAT YOU GIVE
It is not what we wish for that comes back to us. It is what we give.

Chapter 13

SELF-CONTROL

If you have self-control, you have the ability to think as you wish to think. Self-control is thought control. You have the power to control your thoughts and direct them toward specific actions. You have the ability to focus like a laser beam and fix your attention on any given situation for whatever length of time you choose.

Self-control is thinking before acting. This prevents impulsive behavior that may have dangerous or negative consequences. If you don't have self-control, you're likely to injure others *and* hurt yourself in the process. The majority of problems that arise in life are caused by lack of self-control. Inmates in prisons lack the necessary self-control to direct their actions in a positive direction.

A successful person controls his spending habits, feelings toward others, and his ability to be persuaded by others unless he wishes to be influenced by them. Those with self-control don't talk too much and do not interrupt others. To have self-control is to recognize your own mistakes and change them, rather than refusing to see the truth about yourself. Self-control means taking responsibility for everything that happens in your life. When you respond to another person who's angry, you don't have self control. That person is dominating you. If you refuse to become angry by responding with unexpected controlled calmness, you are dominating them.

Self-control is a highly organized function of the mind. It's the ability to make choices about how you behave and act rather than relying on impulses. Instead of acting on instinct or immediate impulse, *pause, evaluate a situation and the consequences that may result* from your behavior—then act.

Self-control is an essential factor in developing personal power. The universe will only give you more when you can handle more. Successful people get high grades on constructively using self-control. Unsuccessful people usually haven't developed this important skill, and therefore the universe will arrange not to give them an increase in things to control.

The art of successful negotiation
grows out of patient
and painstaking self-control.

**Thoughts are
habits in your mind
reproduced in your
physical world.**

Chapter 14

HOW DO I SPEED UP MY SUCCESS?

It's so simple you won't believe it. Nature's principles are always based on simplicity. Three easy, powerful, and fun techniques can propel you towards your goals.

1) Picture your success.

Consciously picture it on a regular basis, with picturing skills anyone can learn. First, why do all this? Is it really necessary? Does it really work? You bet! Successful people always picture success in their minds, consciously or unconsciously.

We've discussed action. This chapter is about mental action, which is the most important action you will take. It makes all other actions more worthwhile and purposeful.

We have two minds: the conscious mind and the subconscious or creative mind. We use the conscious mind to make decisions and think. When we sleep at night, it sleeps. But we also have a subconscious mind that never sleeps, and this creative mind receives the benefit of our picturing. It is in total control of our lives. When the subconscious mind is programmed to accomplish something, it will arrange the universe to create, attract, and manifest those things in your life.

Your life was programmed from the moment you were born. Your subconscious mind is far superior to the most sophisticated computer and stores billions of bits of information. Your parents, siblings, friends and teachers have contributed to your programming. Let me congratulate you on being 100% totally successful according to what was programmed in your subconscious mind. It has created what you are today. Your imagination is a mind power you can begin using NOW. You already visualize every day, every minute. You're thinking thoughts with pictures, that's what visualizing is. We never outgrow our picturing power. We simply need to *take control* of it.

How can you get more? How can

you improve or change your monetary status? How can you improve your relationships? *By changing the programming on your computer!* By placing specific thoughts and pictures in your mind that include the emotions you'd feel if you'd already reached your goal, you program your subconscious mind to make this a reality. This precious sentence is worth rereading!

The super secret here (and this works whether you know the super secret or not) is that the subconscious mind doesn't know the difference between something that's real and *something you imagine with feeling.*

It's a fact that you will not change your life unless you change the pictures in your imagination. You use your conscious mind to program your subconscious mind.

Can you do it? Without a doubt! Thought is the only thing over which you have absolute and complete control. Thought is your most important tool; the one with which you can shape your worldly destiny according to your own choosing. Will you do it? That's up to you.

Napoleon Hill has one basic concept in all of his teachings: "Whatever the *mind*

can conceive and believe, it can achieve."
Napoleon Hill tells us that first we have to
conceive. You conceive by thinking and
feeling as though your definite chief has
already been accomplished. You must *ex-
perience* it as though you are *in the picture* rather than seeing yourself in a photo-
graph. Do this on a regular basis before
you go to sleep at night *and* whenever else
you get a free moment. The more you give
orders to your subconscious mind, the
quicker you will reach your goal.

2) Be careful of what you say!

What you say is what you get. You
command your success through words.
Your words and thoughts have power.
Keep your words and your mental pictures
consistent with your goals. Verbally de-
clare only the good you want, rather than
continuing to talk about what you don't
want.

You can also benefit by controlling
your inner dialogue, or self-talk. A person
can begin asserting control over every
other dimension of his or her life by
speaking words of success to himself and
others. The most damaging words you

will ever hear will come from yourself. Your self-talk can determine the quality of your emotional life. The words you say to yourself determine your attitude and future actions.

Decide to be cheerful and resist every temptation to respond negatively to events in your life. Whatever you say to yourself or others is impressed deeply into your subconscious mind and is likely to be repeated and become a permanent part of life.

Whenever you find a negative statement slipping out of your mouth act as though you didn't say it. Immediately replace it with a more appropriate comment. When others say something negative to you, quickly change what was said by saying a positive to yourself. Then, remove the toxic people from your life as quickly as you can!

3) Handwritten affirmations create a special power in your life.

Why do they work? Because handwritten statements create a clean mental picture of what you want in your creative mind and reinforce your mental images.

Write your affirmations within the thirty minutes before you go to bed. Your creative mind is like a sponge during that time. When you go to sleep your subconscious mind—the one that never sleeps—will keep working on what you just programmed into it.

Your creative mind will create negative as well as positive events. It takes orders from you and is non-judgmental. It doesn't have common sense; it's like a computer. What you put in is what you get out. Your creative mind is a goal machine. It must be programmed by your conscious mind. The thirty minutes before you go to bed is when your subconscious mind is most fertile and receptive. Keep an affirmation notebook by your bedside and make it a habit to write affirmations that evoke emotions about your goals.

If you want things to be different, and you do—or you wouldn't have bought this book—you must *do* something different. Decide right now to speak only positive statements about your goals, to consciously imagine your desires with intense emotion, and to write affirmations about them nightly. If not now, when? Never? Let this be the day. You have the secrets. Successful people use them. They actually *do* what unsuccessful people don't want to do—and *so can you!*

Man's mind once
s t r e t c h e d
by a new idea,
never regains
its original dimensions.

Oliver Wendell Holmes

The brain is as strong as its weakest think.

Eleanor Doan

A man is what he thinks about 24 hours a day.

Ralph Waldo Emerson

You'll never
know your
capacity
until you mix
your efforts
with
imagination.

Chapter 15

HABITS

It is not the understanding of the principles, but the living of them that makes the difference.

A habit is a mental path over which our actions have traveled for some time, each passing making the path a little deeper and wider. Napoleon Hill

Through habits, man shapes his success. A habit grows out of doing the same thing, thinking the same thoughts, or repeating the same words over and over again. A habit can take hold of your mind as easily as it influences the muscles of your body. After a habit has been established it will automatically control and direct the activities of your life.

Habits can be like chains that keep you from the success you want, or instruments that propel you quickly toward your desires.

When you discover a destructive habit, you can consciously direct your thoughts and your efforts to change it.

You may find that you have some habits to remove and some habits to create based on an evaluation of each of the success habits in this booklet. Old unproductive habits can be removed by simply creating a new pathway in your thoughts that will lead to new actions.

Habits are thoughts produced in your physical world. A habit is the mental blueprint or path you follow. When you begin a new habit, focus your conscious attention on building a new mental path. (Concentration is nothing more than control of attention). The more frequently you use the new habit, the sooner it will become worn and easily traveled. Using the success habits in each chapter, focus on creating one new habit each month. Resist the temptation to travel the old road if you're incorporating a new habit. Soon, your conscious attention will become unconscious and you'll automatically use habits of success to bring you to your goals!

IF IT'S GOING TO BE...

IT'S
UP TO ME!

Glenda Feilen

CAN HELP YOU

Glenda Feilen, author and lecturer, nutritional expert, international marketing director, and mother of five shares techniques that you can incorporate in your life to achieve your relationship, prosperity, and success dreams.

Get what you want

Do what you want

Be what you want

BODY CLUES

YOUR BODY SHAPE shapes your personality

By Glenda Feilen

THREE NO-FAIL TECHNIQUES

Any of which can change your life forever!

Glenda Feilen + = change your life forever!

By Glenda Feilen

Are All Your Pieces in Place?

by Glenda Feilen

A Mortal's Guide to Success, Joy and Happiness

Schedule a

PUT YOUR PIECES IN PLACE

WORKSHOP

Transform your life by attending a exhilarating, fun, life-changing workshop.

ARE YOUR PIECES IN PLACE WORKBOOK

Let Glenda personally guide you in your
life transformation.

(available soon!)

Contact us:
www.areallyourpiecesinplace.com

STARQUEST INC.
P.O. Box 2218
El Cajon, CA 92021